FOR IT IS BY GRACE

BURL L. SHEPARD

Words Matter Publishing
P.O. Box 531
Salem, Il 62881
www.wordsmatterpublishing.com

ISBN 13: 978-1-953912-40-4

Library of Congress Catalog Card Number: 2021949713

TABLE OF CONTENTS

CHAPTER 1

One of the first places many non-believers go when presented with the Gospel is evolution. Perhaps there are reasons to consider both evolution and the biblical account of creation. While there is no room for compromise in regard to God's word, it is conceivable the issue of evolution can be approached from a biblical point of view. Doing this might cause more people to seek God and perhaps find Him.

Around 6,000 years is the most-used number for the biblical age of the earth. In 2 Peter 3:8 (NIV) we read, "With the Lord a day is like a thousand years and a thousand years are like a day." We are dealing with great mystery when we deal with God. The Bible says God created the earth and all things, including man, in six days. He rested on the seventh day.

The scientific age of the Earth is between four and five billion years. There are many in the scientific community who subscribe to the Big Bang Theory. This theory can be intriguing when used with the assumption the cause and effect were controlled by God. The following briefly focuses on the Big Bang Theory, using the hypothesis it was God-controlled.

In total darkness a tiny sphere was lovingly crafted. The mass of the sphere was incredible, for within it was placed everything that exists in the universe. The Godhead spoke. A fathomless explosion occurred. Everything from within the sphere was strewn outwardly in all directions, a powerful wave of everything from which the universe was formed. The wave still continues on its outward journey of expansion. This was done through God the Son. "In the beginning, was the Word, and the Word was with God, and the Word was God. He was with God in the beginning. Through Him all things were made; without Him nothing was made that has been made. (John 1 : 1-3 NIV)

The special planet Earth was crafted by the Godhead, again through God the Son. The Godhead watched and controlled as the planet's evolution made progress. From deep within the earth, water formed and flowed toward the surface. A variety of plant life appeared and flourished. Prehistoric creatures, including manlike creatures, roamed the Earth. The manlike creatures had no relationship to man, for they did not contain a soul, and relied entirely on animal instinct.

Through means of a natural disaster, the Godhead destroyed all life. Again, the Godhead watched and controlled as the planet evolved, this time into placid, tranquil serenity. Then, "The Lord God formed the man from the dust of the ground and breathed into his nostrils the breath of life, and the man became a living being." (Genesis 2:7 NIV). The first man, Adam, was placed in the Garden of Eden. The first woman, Eve, was then formed from the man's rib.

There are three theories about the fate of the universe in regard to the Big Bang Theory. One is that it will continue to expand forever. The second is that a time will come when it will lose the force that was created by the explosion, causing it to go flat. This would cause the stars and all other matter to die. It would thus become a dead universe. The third theory, which is intriguing, is that the universe will reach a certain point in its expansion, then reverse course and come back against itself. This theory supports the biblical account that the time is coming when the skies will roll back, and God will create a new Heaven and a new Earth.

"Then I saw a new heaven and a new earth for the first heaven and the first earth had passed away, and there was no longer any sea." (Revelation 21:1 NIV).

The Big Bang Theory would explain evidence including manlike found of dinosaurs and other prehistoric creatures. It also would have no bearing on the biblical account of Noah and the flood. While it can be fascinating to ponder God's creation of the heavens and Earth as well as other mysteries concerning Him, do these things really matter as we go about our daily lives? How God did these things should not be our main concern. In regard to the scheme of things concerning God's plan during our physical lives our main objective should be to seek God and the free gift He offers all people though the sacrificial blood of God the Son.

Author's Note

General information in regard to The Big Bang Theory came from the book Cosmic Dispatches. The book was taken from writings of six authors over a period of several years. It was edited by John Noble Wilford. The idea of this being God-controlled was my own.

CHAPTER 2

We live in a fallen world and are separated from God and his goodness. There is nothing that is not touched by the evilness of the world. All things in which mankind is involved are saturated by the worldly sins of self, sex, power and wealth. One only needs to consider the countless number of lawsuits directed toward churches, schools and other institutions and organizations because of sexual abuse to reach this conclusion. Ample evidence is also found in the political world, for there too the evilness abounds. The only glimmer of hope is provided by those who have been saved from sin by the grace of God and who are themselves sinners, but have the spirit of God living within.

What is this grace of God? What does it mean, and how do we receive it? First, we must understand that God's way is the example of what our morals should be. It is God's law that makes us conscious of sin (Romans

3:20). Without this, people are left to create their own version of good and evil, which is now the situation multitudes face. So, we must start with God's law. Remember, whatever you allow to come before God is your god. Exodus 20:3-17 outlines the foundation of God's law:

THE TEN COMMANDMENTS

You shall have no other gods before Me.
You shall not make for yourself an idol in the form of anything.

You shall not misuse the name of the Lord your God.

Remember the Sabbath day by keeping it holy.

Honor your father and your mother.

You shall not murder.

You shall not commit adultery.

You shall not steal.

You shall not give false testimony.

You shall not covet.

God wants parents to teach their children His law. But first, the parents must know and observe the law themselves. The family unit is the structure that holds this country together, but for years it has been under attack by those who are of the world. Single parents, divorce, and abortion are tearing this country apart. One might conclude they probably wouldn't be able to follow God's set of laws all of the time and wonder why they should even try, being certain in their mind it would be too difficult to receive His grace. Part of that reasoning would be correct, the part about not being able to always obey God's law. The part about His grace being too difficult to receive is incorrect. Why?It is because when you know God's law, and become conscious of the fact that in His eyes you are a sinner, if you ask for His forgiveness, you will receive it. You are saved by His grace alone, not by trying to obey His laws, for there will be moments when you fail. Receiving God's grace is not at all difficult. The difficult part for many people is arriving at the point of realizing His grace is something they need.

One might wonder what the advantage would be of following the law God has ordained. It is important to understand that God's ways are in stark contrast to the ways of the world. His honesty is absolute. For example, we see and hear advertisements for products supposedly so close to perfection that there is only a 1/10 of 1% chance of failure. And there are many medications and medical products that list so many possible side effects, including death, that one's head starts to spin. The point is that the people behind these advertisements are leaving themselves a way out in case of failure.

There are two words I have from time to time found to be problematic. The first is the word "but", as in, "I thought your battery was fine, (but) it won't hold a charge. You'll have to purchase a new one." So, I then find my carefully planned day unexpectedly interrupted, and the culprit to be the problematic "but". And this word "but", when used in conjunction with the second problematic word, which is "unfortunately", can really be bad. An example of the two words joining forces – "I'm sorry sir, we really thought the information from your damaged phone could be transferred to the one you just purchased (but unfortunately…) and then comes a lot of technical language that I don't understand as to why the information can't be transferred, and my tired brain and churning stomach just wants to escape to fresh air and sunshine.

Unlike the dealings of the world, you will not be forgiven 99.9% but 100%. God will not leave Himself a way out. Nor will you hear from Him "Ok, I'll forgive you now (but)", or the really bad one, "(but unfortunately), I'll be watching everything you do. Don't make me have to take your salvation back." No, He will not speak with you in variation or with nuance. He will, however, see everything you do and know everything you think as He does with all people, for He is God. "For a man's ways are in full view of the Lord, and he examines all his paths" (Proverbs 5:21 NIV). Nothing has changed as far as His knowledge of you. And what are the side effects? Your understanding of God and the love He has for you will grow, and as time passes, God will bring about a desire within you to please Him. But there's much more than this, for at the death of the physical body all believers immediately enter into eternal life and experience existence the way it was meant to be, for they are no longer separated from God.

But one might wonder how this could be, God saving them by His grace without threat of punishment for future sins. We start with the Trinity, the union of three, the Father, the Son and the Hold Spirit in one Godhead. This has been described as the threefold personality of the one Divine Being. The Trinity is one of the great mysteries of God, for He exists as one but also three at the same time.

CHAPTER 3

In Genesis Chapter 3, we can read the account of Eve's encounter with the devil. After placing Adam and Eve in the garden, God told them they must not eat fruit from the tree that was in the middle of the garden, or they would die. The devil, in his craftiness, persuaded Eve this was not so, telling her if she ate of the fruit, she would be like God, gaining wisdom and knowing good and evil. Eve took some fruit and ate it, and then gave some to her husband, Adam. This resulted in the fall of mankind, as all descendants of the first man and the first woman were then destined to be born into sin. But, because of God's great love of the world, He devised a plan for mankind's redemption. God the Son was born as a human, was subject to all the temptations of mankind, yet lived the perfect, sinless life. He was betrayed by one of His disciples and taken to be crucified. God the Son was the sacrificial lamb of

God the Father, dying for the sins of all mankind so that any person who believed in Him might also live. "For God so loved the world that He gave His one and only son, that whoever believes in Him shall not perish but have eternal life. For God did not send His son into the world to condemn the world, but to save the world through Him" (John 3:16-17 NIV). This is a free gift to all who would receive it. "For it is by grace you have been saved, through faith – and this not from yourselves, it is the gift of God – not by works, so that no one can boast." (Ephesians 2:8 NIV).

There is a term, "may your soul rest in peace," for those who have died. This is not a biblical term, nor is it accurate. For those who have accepted Christ as Lord, the death of the physical body has nothing to do with resting. Your soul is not resting in a state of unknowing sleep, but has become more alive and active than it has ever been, for at death the soul is released from its bondage to the physical realm. The promise of Jesus is a real, living, peaceful rest believers experience after death. "Come to me, all you who are weary and burdened, and I will give you rest. Take my yoke upon you and learn from me, for I am gentle and humble in heart, and you will find rest in your souls. For my yoke is easy and my burden is light." (Matthew 11:28-30 NIV). "He who dwells in the shelter (presence) of the Most High will rest in the shadow of the Almighty." (Psalm 91:1-2 NIV). Those who die without accepting Christ will not find peace. "'There is no peace', says my God, for the wicked." (Isaiah 57:21 NIV).

In a previous statement, I made the remark that receiving God's grace is not difficult. The difficult part is realizing just how much you need Him. The journey to find God is often not easy. The following poem is a testament to this:

Oh, long and dark the stairs I trod,

With stumbling feet to find my God

Gaining a foothold bit by bit,

Then slipping back and losing it.

Never progressing, striving still

With weakening grasp and fainting will.

Bleeding to climb to God, while He

Serenely smiled, unnoting me.

Then came a certain time when I

Loosened my hold and fell thereby.

Down to the lowest step my fall,

As if I had not climbed at all.

And while I lay despairing there,

I heard a footfall on the stair,

In the same path where I, dismayed

Faltered and fell and lay afraid,

And lo! When hope had ceased to be

My God came down the stairs to me.

Author Unknown

CHAPTER 4

If you reach the point of realizing there's no place to turn except to God, how does one proceed? You may be familiar with His word through church and reading the Bible, or you may have very little knowledge of Him. It doesn't matter. Let's turn to the Apostle Paul. He was not one of the original twelve disciples. In fact, Paul, who was at first called Saul, never saw Jesus in the flesh. The man Saul hated those who believed in Jesus. "But Saul began to destroy the church. Going from house to house, he dragged off men and women and placed them in prison." (Acts 8:3 NIV). Saul was responsible for the death of many Christians. However, while traveling to the synagogues in Damascus to search them for believers in Jesus, he encountered a light from Heaven. A voice, identifying himself as Jesus, gave Saul instructions on what to do when he reached Damascus. Saul was to contact a man called Ananias. Before Saul's arrival, Ananias had a vision from Heaven in which he was told, "This man is my chosen instrument to carry my name before the Gentiles and their kings and before the people of Israel, I will show him how much he must suffer for my name." (Acts 9:15-16 NIV). After the encounter with the light from Heaven, his meeting with Ananias, and finally gaining the confidence of the fearful believers, Saul was known as Paul.

In 2 Corinthians 12:1-4, Paul writes about what today might be called an out of body experience, in which he heard inexpressible things; things that man is not permitted to tell. We can believe these words are true when Paul writes, "I want you to know, brothers, that the gospel I preached is not something that man made up. I did not receive it from any man, nor was I taught it; rather I received it by revelation from Jesus Christ." (Galatians 1:11-12 NIV). Paul has been credited with writing thirteen of the twenty-seven books that are contained in the New Testament. While this cannot be 100% confirmed, Paul's influence on Christianity cannot be denied. His teachings contain the formula for receiving God's grace. "If you confess with your mouth Jesus is Lord, and believe in your heart that God raised him from the dead, you will be saved. For it is with your heart that you believe and are justified, and it is with your mouth that you confess and are saved." (Romans 10:9-10 NIV).

If you do this, you will have the third personality of the Trinity, God the Holy Spirit, living within. For Jesus said, "And I will ask the Father, and he will give you another Counselor to be with you forever – the Spirit of Truth. The world cannot accept him, because it neither sees him nor knows him. But you know him, for he lives with you and will be in you." (John 14:16-17 NIV). And what is the difference between you and the world now that you have accepted Christ? As time passes and you grow in faith, you will see a great contrast between your way of thinking and the thinking of those without the Spirit. "The man without the Spirit does not accept the things that come from the Spirit of God, for they are foolishness to him, and he cannot understand them, because they are spiritually discerned." (1 Corinthians 2:14 NIV).

It is important to realize, once you have received God's grace, you will never lose it. As an example, consider alcohol or drug abuse. If, in your despair, you cried out in sincerity for God's forgiveness and help, you will have Him during your darkest moments. While it is possible for God to heal any infirmity, whether a physical condition or a moral weakness, this is not always His way. He may instead work through the Holy Spirit that now lives within you, and you may find the strength to fight harder against your bondage. A person might also be led to seek help from sources they would not have before finding God. No matter the outcome, His love and grace will be with you always.

And what of the person that accepts Christ and moves on to live what they consider to be a strong Christian life, but one day they falter, and commit a sin either by thought or deed? Should they, in trembling fear, beg for God's forgiveness? While they did not receive a free pass from God in regard to the occurrence, why ask for something that is already possessed - God's forgiveness? As they consider the fact that their sins are covered, their eyes should well up with tears as they realize the magnitude of what Jesus did for them by His crucifixion. Then, they should talk to the One who made them, not to ask for something they already possess, but for the strength and wisdom to move forward, a stronger person in Christ, as they look toward the time that they will be made perfect in God's holy presence.

CHAPTER 5

As the Christian cannot live the perfect life, neither will life be perfect for the Christian. While those who are saved by God's grace know He is real, one must understand, so too is the devil. Revelation chapter 12:7-9 gives the account of great war in Heaven when Satan and his angels rebelled against God. This resulted in Satan and his followers being cast from Heaven to Earth. As long as the Christian is in the physical body, they are separated from God's presence and must constantly fight against spiritual attacks from Satan and his fallen angels. Only when believers depart the body at death will they be freed from these spiritual assaults. The apostle Paul fully understood the spiritual attacks, for he too experienced them, and described the believer's plight in this way: "But one thing I do: Forgetting what is behind and straining toward what is ahead, I press on toward the goal to win the prize for which God has called me heavenward in Christ Jesus." (Philippians 3:13-14 NIV).

Satan, through his deceptiveness, causes much grief. The apostle Paul gives birth to this through his writings. "For Satan himself masquerades as an angel of light. It is not surprising, then, if his servants masquerade as servants of righteousness. Their end will be what their actions deserve." (2 Corinthians 11:14-15 NIV). From time to time, we hear accounts of people who were supposedly people of God, and who had a very large following of the faithful. Through some type of revelation, these individuals were exposed to be imposters, interested only in the sins of the world – self, sex, power and wealth. They will receive their just reward. Their only hope would be sincere repentance to God. Sadly, this type of transgression causes much distress and soul-searching from the people who believed in them.

CHAPTER 6

We all suffer hardships and need God's spiritual help as we make our way through this life. Sometimes, these occurrences inspire people in ways that give strength to others. Thomas A. Dorsey was an African American man born in 1899 in Villa Rica, GA. While pastoring a church he lost his wife during childbirth, and the baby boy shortly after her death. This tragic event inspired him to write the lyrics to a beautiful song which has helped many people: "Precious Lord: take my hand, lead me on, help me stand. I am tired, I am weak, I am worn. Through the storm, through the night, lead me on to the light. Take my hand, precious Lord, lead me home."

There is also a literal example of the theme of the song, ages before it was written, in the account of Jesus walking on the water. After the feeding of the 5,000 with the five loaves of bread and two fish, Jesus sent His disciples by boat to the other side of the lake, telling them He would join them soon. (Matthew 14: 15-21). Jesus then went alone to a secluded area to pray. When he returned to the waterside, Jesus saw that while the boat was a considerable distance from land, the disciples had not reached the far shore because of a strong wind. Jesus then went out to them, walking upon the water of the lake. When the disciples saw Him, they were terrified, thinking it was a ghost. Jesus then identified Himself, telling the disciples not to fear. Peter, who was one of the first two disciples chosen by Jesus, cried out, "Lord if it is you tell me to come to you on the water," to which Jesus replied, "Come" (Matthew 14:28-29 NIV). Peter started to walk toward Jesus, but when confronted by the wind and rough water he was afraid and started to sink. Peter cried out for the Lord to save him. Jesus reached out and took hold of Peter's hand which prevented him from sinking beneath the water. After they climbed into the boat, the wind died down. These events caused the disciples to realize that Jesus truly was the Son of God (Matthew 14:29-33).

What of the disciples of Jesus? What was their fate? Of the twelve disciples, the Bible tells of the death of two. Judas, who betrayed Jesus for thirty silver coins, felt remorse when he saw that Jesus was condemned, for he realized he had betrayed innocent blood. He tried to return the silver coins to the chief priests and elders, but they refused to accept them. So, Judas threw the money into the temple, and went away and hanged himself. (Matthew 27: 3-5). Also, around that time King Herod arrested some who belonged to the church, and had James, the brother of John put to death with the sword. The Bible doesn't tell if James' death was from a piercing wound or if he was beheaded. (Acts 12:1-2). According to church tradition, the Apostle Peter was crucified with his head downward, and the apostle Paul was beheaded. It is believed Paul was not crucified because he was a Roman citizen. Thus, in this way, the truth of Jesus was sealed with the blood of Peter and Paul.

The disciples of Jesus, while on the Earth, had nothing to gain by their faith in Him. Their only reward was continuous persecution by the leaders of that time. But the power of God held them together and gave them strength when they most needed it. The Bible has withstood the test of time. Those who dispute its truth have but a limited number of years to make their determination. Then, they are suddenly gone. While they have a soul, during their time on Earth they rely only on animal instinct, as did the manlike creatures of ages past, and after they are gone, leave behind a legacy of irrelevant speculation. "Why, you do not even know what will happen tomorrow. What is your life? You are a mist that appears for a little while, then vanishes." (James 4:14 NIV).

On the other hand, God has ruled with absolute sovereignty throughout the ages, touching all people in the same way. Many times, a sermon or song from years past produce the same effect in the heart today as it did when first communicated. "Since ancient times no one has heard, no ear has perceived, no eye has seen any God besides You, who acts on behalf of those who wait for Him." (Isaiah 64:4 NIV). The mysteries of God are abundant. Peter was a man who walked alongside Jesus, looked into His eyes, saw the miracles He performed, took hold of His hand while on the water to keep from sinking beneath the waves, and saw the crucifixion. Yet, in his remarks about the letters of the Apostle Paul, Peter makes the statement that parts of the letters are hard to understand, which leaves an opening for irresponsible people to distort their meaning. In 2Peter 3:16, Peter says we must be on guard, and not drawn away from the truth of God.

CHAPTER 7

At the start of your day, push the re-set button God has given you - prayer. First, He is worthy of your worship. Secondly, prayers will help you to focus on the notable things of your life. It is essential to have honest, straightforward conversations with God. You should be able to talk to Him about any subject. Also, not to be overlooked is the importance of the Lord's Prayer. Jesus instructed that prayer should not be numerous words of repetition. And, in regard to the Lord's Prayer, He said God knows what we need before we ask. For that reason, there is a difference between the two methods of prayer. When we use our own words, we are asking for what we want. When we say the Lord's Prayer, we are asking for what God knows we need. There may be times when what we want and what God knows we need will be different. Only He knows what the future holds, and the different paths we need to travel in order to fulfill His purpose for our lives. Romans 12:12 reminds us:

Be joyful in hope,

Patient in affliction,

Faithful in prayer.

The Lord's Prayer

Our Father which art in Heaven, Hallowed be thy name.

Thy kingdom come. Thy will be done on Earth, as it is in Heaven.

Give us this day our daily bread.

And forgive us our debts, as we forgive our debtors.

And lead us not into temptation, but deliver us from evil: For thine is the kingdom, and the power, and the glory, forever. Amen

Matthew 6:9-13, King James Version

Part of the Lord's Prayer describes two kinds of forgiveness, God forgiving us for our transgressions, and our own forgiveness of those who do wrong toward us. Bestowing forgiveness can be difficult to accomplish. There are those who spend a lifetime living in bitterness while searching for the strength to forgive someone who has betrayed or done harm, either to themselves or to a loved one. We are all human, and one may never be able to fully accomplish this while living our physical lives. However, one might approach this difficult matter from the perspective that all people are susceptible to the spiritual attacks from Satan and his forces. Thus, by being able to better understand what influenced the perpetrator to carry out the transgression, some degree of peace might be found, along with a feeling of compassion toward the one that committed the offense.

CHAPTER 8

There are many problems facing America today, including social, moral, and political upheaval. It is certain we are living in unprecedented times, and one wonders if the country will survive the ongoing onslaught. There are many in foreign countries as well as here at home that wish for American's demise. It would be tragic to lose our freedom because of those whose god is the world and its evilness.

The following excerpt is an excellent example of a solution to the problems we face: "Spaceship earth came with its own set of instructions; it is called the Holy Bible. And, if it were not divinely inspired, it would still be the best blueprint for an orderly existence." (Jim Davidson - Column #746). While the Bible is divinely inspired, "All scripture is God-breathed" (2Timothy 3:16 NIV), it is also true that no other precepts exist that would promote peace and harmony as does the word of God, a faultless example being: "Each of you should look not only to your own interest, but also to the interest of others." (Philippians 2:4 NIV). Along with that, add this short passage of Scripture: "A gentle answer turns away wrath, but a harsh word stirs up anger." (Proverbs 15:1 NIV). These are common-sense behaviors given through God the Holy Spirit. The problem is, there are those throughout the world who want to control the general population in order to fulfill their own selfish desires. These are people who live without the Spirit of God, and therefore belong to the world.

We must realize we are all one race, descendants of Adam, and after the flood, of Noah and his three sons. The Bible speaks of equality when speaking of humankind: "Then Peter began to speak: I now realize how true it is that God does not show favoritism but accepts men from every nation who fear Him and do what is right." (Acts 10:34-35 NIV). And also: "The God who made the world and everything in it is the Lord of Heaven and Earth and does not live in temples built by hands. And he is not served by human hands, as if he needed anything, because he himself gives all men life and breath and everything else. From one man he made every nation of men, that they should inhabit the whole earth; and he determined the times set for them and the exact places where they should live." (Acts 17:24-26 NIV).

I've never been comfortable with the term person of color in regard to an African American person. While I see nothing disrespectful in using the stereotypical term, an old Sunday School song might help to explain my reasoning. "Jesus loves the little children. All the children of the world. Red, brown, yellow. Black and white. They are precious in His sight. Jesus loves the little children of the world." We are all people of color. Every race in its own way is unique, just as every person in their own way is unique, according to God's workmanship.

I can remember the feeling of satisfaction I experienced whenever I sent a basketball flying toward a hoop, and on occasion, watched as it fell through. And on rarer occasions, I received the same feeling of satisfaction when, upon rolling a bowling ball, I saw all the pins at the end of the alley scatter. But sadly, I could never achieve the same results after every attempt. This troubled me, for as I reflected on the matter I wondered why, if I was able to do this after one attempt, my body wouldn't retain the information it used for that success, therefore making it possible for me to be successful after every attempt.

After more thought in regard to this, I realized my human flaws prevented me from making the selfsame movements on every attempt, with either the basketball or bowling ball. I then realized a robot could do this, for only a machine could be programmed to make the identical movements necessary to achieve the same results in a perpetual manner. This led to the thought that God could have programmed humankind as robots, ready to do His bidding without using the faculty of thinking. Instead, He gave us free will. Though we live in a world of multiple and diverse situations, God has given us the ability to make our own decisions as we travel the different pathways of our lives. The choices we make affect us and others in a multitude of consequential ways.

CHAPTER 9

Not all sins are equal. It is obvious to the rational thinker that by using ordinal numbers given to us by God, the commandment "You shall not murder" ranks above the commandment "You shall not give false testimony." However, both are sins, requiring God's forgiveness through the blood of Jesus. Let's take a hypothetical situation to expand on this. Some might think that in today's world, the following could not be possible, but in fact there are countries such as China and Iran in which the following, in some form, does occur.

Imagine an apartment containing a number of Christians. Upon hearing a loud knock, one of those inside the apartment opens the door revealing several government officials. There is a particular person among the Christians the government officials want to take into custody for interrogation. It so happens the person they are searching for is hidden away in a secret place within the apartment. Do the Christians, in order to keep from breaking the commandment, "You shall not give false testimony," reveal the hiding place of the one sought by the government officials, knowing the person would be tortured and possibly killed, or do they call upon the concepts of common sense and choices given them by God, and tell the government officials the one they are searching for is not there? The answer should be obvious.

The following two passages of Scripture might be called a paradox, for they appear to contradict each other but actually express the truth. "So, we fix our eyes not on what is seen, but on what is unseen. For what is seen is temporary, but what is unseen is eternal." (2Corinthians 4:18 NIV). And: "The heavens declare the glory of God; the skies proclaim the works of His hands. Day after day they pour forth speech; night after night they display knowledge. There is no speech or language where their voice is not heard. Their voice goes out into all the earth, their words to the ends of the world." (Psalm 19:1-4 NIV). On one hand, we are told to look to the unseen spiritual world to find true meaning, and on the other hand to search God's physical works. In actuality, all concepts were created by

God. Whether driven by faith or driven by science, He is the Creator of all things. "For by Him all things were created: things in Heaven and on Earth, visible and invisible." (Colossians 1:16 NIV).

Thought is a God-given concept that parallels free will, for what we do with our thoughts defines our lives. We all start with the God-given concept of agnosticism. Then, we must choose between the God-given concept of faith and the God-given concept of atheism. All things, whether material-related or thought-related were created by God. Our thoughts can take us to heights of Godly spirituality. Thoughts can also drive us to the depths of Satanic depravity, for a human being is capable of doing anything the mind can bring forth. As an example, bondage to pornography can by degrees bring about desires for more extreme sexual experiences which can lead to un-natural sexual interests and acts such as child pornography and bestiality.

I can recall watching a commercial that aired on television several years ago, in which a clip from an old silent movie was used. In the scene the heroine in the film was captured by the villain, then bound, gagged, and placed across a set of rails. The villain then boarded an unoccupied locomotive and pulled back on the throttle to start the locomotive moving toward the helpless woman. With an evil smile upon his face, the villain leapt from the locomotive and stood watching as it rolled slowly toward the heroine. The poor lady lay wide-eyed, terrified as the slow-moving locomotive sped toward her.

This too is a paradox, for while it might be considered an absurd statement to say the slow-moving locomotive was speeding toward the frightened lady, from her perspective it was certainly approaching at a high rate of speed. The hero of the film, who was on a distant rise watching what was unfolding through field glasses, also had an impression of speed from the slow-moving locomotive. Fortunately, he arrived seconds before the slow-moving locomotive reached the lady and carried her to safety. The hero then captured the villain and tied him securely. I'm certain he and the lady took the villain to the nearest law enforcement establishment and are now living happily ever after.

An analogy similar to this can be used to describe humankind, for while, especially in our younger years, it seems that our lives will never end, but in reality, when compared to eternity, our physical lives exist but a moment. As we grow older, we learn the truth of the following passage: "All men are like grass, and all their glory is like the flowers of the field; the grass withers and the flower fall, but the word of the Lord stands forever." (1Peter 1:24-25 NIV). Just as the slow-moving locomotive was speeding toward the lady on the tracks, our seemingly slow-moving lives are speeding toward eternity.

Another interesting analogy can be made between snowflakes and humankind. It has been said, of the trillions of snowflakes that fall at any given time, no two are alike. They maneuver about the currents of air going hither and thither as they make their perilous journey to the earth. The silent beauty of fallen snow cannot be ignored, and the benefits are many. Snow that has fallen conserves moisture in the soil, and provides protection for plant life as it insulates from extreme cold. This is one of God's physical laws at work.

Much the same can be said about people, for like snowflakes, no two are alike. Every human being is unique in appearance as well as character. And like the snowflakes, many perilous paths are taken as they journey through life. There is much imperfection in the world, for we are fallen people. But like the snow, quiet beauty also exists. Watching a small child who is deep in imaginative play is an example. So too is the love we feel when holding a newborn child or grandchild securely in our arms. I believe these moments are as close to understanding God's love as we will ever be. This is an example of God's spiritual laws at work.

What is the purpose of our physical lives? It is a quest to seek God, and hopefully find Him. Humankind has shown a remarkable ability for making this more difficult than it is. Eternal life awaits only the asking, a free gift for all who accept Christ as Lord of their lives. Why did Jesus begin his life on Earth as a newborn baby? Why didn't he begin as a young man and immediately deliver his message? It was because Jesus wanted to experience the whole of human existence from the womb to death. This reality makes what he did for humankind all the more incredible.

CHAPTER 10

There are those who say The Old Testament is not important, and does not need to be read or studied. However, God loves all people, and started to reveal his plan for the redemption of humankind soon after the fall occurred in the Garden of Eden. To the devil God said: "And I will put enmity between you and the woman, and between your offspring and hers; he will crush your head, and you will strike his heel." (Genesis 3:15 NIV). This passage is often referred to as the First Gospel. *You will strike his heel* referred to Satan's repeated attempts to defeat Christ during his life on earth. *He will crush your head* foreshadows Satan's defeat when Jesus rose from the dead, for by his resurrection Satan no longer had power over death. From that moment forward the Old Testament repeatedly makes reference to Jesus and the salvation He will offer humanity. While the Book of Revelation is not in the

Old Testament, it gives certainty to its importance with these words: "For the essence of prophecy is to give a clear witness for Jesus." (Revelation 19:10 NIV). The New Testament is sprinkled throughout with references from the Old Testament in regard to Jesus. To ignore the Old Testament is to ignore the very foundation of the gospel.

Even though Jesus overcame Satan's power over death, Satan is still the ruler of the Earth and will continue to be until he meets his doom and faces the Last Judgement. Michael is the mighty Archangel of God. When Satan and his angels rebelled against God in Heaven, Michael is referred to as the leader of God's angels during the battle in which Satan and his followers were cast to the Earth. (Revelation 12:7-9). Daniel 12:1 indicates Michael protected the Israelite nation from spiritual attack. However, "even the archangel Michael, when he was disputing with the devil about the body of Moses, did not dare to condemn him but said 'The Lord rebuke you.'" (Jude 1:9 NIV). The devil is indeed a powerful being, but he is confined within the boundaries God has set for him.

The following passage of Scripture is very important to understand. Focus on it and let it permeate your mind as you fully grasp its marvelous meaning: "I am the resurrection and the life. He who believes in Me will live, even though he dies; and whoever lives and believes in Me will never die." (John 11:25-26 NIV). The Message interprets it in this way: "You don't have to wait for the end of time for resurrection. I am, right now, resurrection and life. The one who believes in Me, even though he or she dies, will live, and everyone who lives believing in Me does not ultimately die at all."

What does this mean? In essence it means that at the moment one accepts Christ as Lord and Savior their soul is assured of eternal life, and at the very moment of death of the physical body the soul immediately enters into Heaven and God's presence independently of the physical body.

There cannot be good without evil for comparison; there cannot be evil without good for comparison, for without both, neither can exist. The same holds true of Heaven and Hell, for how can one be described without the existence of the other? God is not the cause of evil, but for his own intention allows evil to occur through Satan. The evilness of the devil increases God's ability to draw people closer to Him and increase their dependence on Him.

It has been said during His ministry Jesus never referred to Himself as being God. However, during the Feast of Dedication at Jerusalem, while walking in the temple, several gathered around him asking questions. At that time Jesus said to them, "I and the Father are one." (John 10:30 NIV). In saying this Jesus was claiming to be not only a teacher of the law but the Supreme Being. This statement resulted in the religious leaders calling for His death, for their laws said anyone claiming to be God should die. In their ignorance and pride, they considered what Jesus said to be a blasphemous statement. They did not realize they were standing before the Son of God. "The Son is the radiance of God's glory and the exact representation of his being, sustaining all things by his powerful word." (Hebrews 1:3 NIV).

CHAPTER 11

There is a famous and very valuable work of art entitled, *The Scream*. It was created by the artist Edvard Munch in the year 1893. It is a painting of a distorted face crying out in agony and terror at the horror of human existence. While this artwork does not have to do with the believer, it should bear heavily upon those who do not accept Christ, for at the death of their physical bodies their soul will hear these words: "You belong to your father the devil, and you want to carry out your father's desire." (John 8:44 NIV). They will then understand the reality of these words: "By myself I have sworn, my mouth has uttered in all integrity a word that will not be revoked: Before me every knee will bow; by me every tongue will swear." (Isaiah 45:23 NIV). Then they will realize the horror of existence without the saving power of the blood of Jesus.

But it will be too late. All that remains is the wrath of God and The Scream.

And what awaits the believer? It is impossible to imagine. "No eye has seen, no ear has heard, no mind has conceived what God has prepared for those who love him." (1Corinthians 2:9 NIV). We have seen but a glimpse of what lies on the other side. "Now we see but a poor reflection as in a mirror; then we shall see face to face. Now I know in part; then I shall know fully, even as I am fully known." (1Corinthians 13:12 NIV). Follow me on an imaginative trip to the other side where we might see God's great love at work.

A small group of children was playing in a beautiful meadow that was sprinkled with brightly colored flowers. Suddenly an angel appeared, his large wings silhouetted against the brightly lit sky. When the children saw the approaching angel, they started screaming as they pointed their fingers in his direction. The angel flew low over the screaming and yelling children, then circled and landed gracefully perhaps thirty feet from them. Still screaming and yelling at the top of their voices, the children ran as fast as their legs would carry them toward the towering angel. It was Michael, God's mighty Archangel, and the smile on his face as he watched the children running toward him would have melted a glacier. When the children reached him, he knelt, engulfing them in his arms and covering them within the folds of his wings.

These were a very small part of God's special children, children who had lost their lives to the sin of abortion, and had been willingly sacrificed to the evil one as a result of lustful pleasures of the flesh. There were countless numbers of these children in Heaven, each receiving loving ministries from God's holy angels. At the proper moment, as they matured spiritually, they would join the general population of Heaven, each being qualified to perform special loving tasks.

The children loved all of the angels, but the mighty warrior angel Michael was their favorite. After the love-filled greetings were finished, Michael interacted with the children playing heavenly versions of croquet, badminton, and tag. How long these activities lasted were not important, for in Heaven time does not exist. Compared to time as it is known on Earth the interactions could have lasted weeks, months, or even years, but in Heaven, when compared to eternity it was no longer than the blink of an eye.

It is important to understand that Jesus is not a created being. God did not create Jesus in order to have a son. Jesus is God, a part of the Trinity having no beginning and no end. Proverbs 8:1-36 has some beautiful passages of Scripture, but they can be confusing. These passages are written in the context of Wisdom, but one could easily believe that some are in regard to Jesus.

Some brief examples of what I am alluding to are: "I love those who love Me, and those who seek Me find Me." (Proverbs 8:17 NIV). "The Lord brought me forth as the first of His works before His deeds of old. I was appointed from eternity, from the beginning, before the world began." (Proverbs 8:22-23 NIV). "For whoever finds Me finds life and receives favor from the Lord. But whoever fails to find Me harms himself; all who hate Me love death." (Proverbs 8:35-36 NIV).

In actuality Jesus and wisdom are one and the same, for wisdom is the foundation for which all things were made. "My purpose is that they may be encouraged in heart and united in love, so that they may hear the full riches of complete understanding, in order that they may know the mysteries of God, namely Christ, in whom are hidden all the treasures of wisdom and knowledge." (Colossians 2:2-3 NIV).

CHAPTER 12

While the word of God can be confusing, even the apostle Peter alluded to this in regard to some of Paul's letters, the Holy Bible was not intended to be a one-time, tell-all, know-all message. It was purposely designed by God to continuously draw us back to its words for reflection and discernment. By doing this, we often reach an "aha" moment in regard to something we had found to be perplexing.

The drawing power of the Bible also prevents us from wandering from God's word and going our own way. After placing Adam in the Garden of Eden, God told him he could eat from any tree in the garden except the tree of the knowledge of good and evil. Adam was told if he did this he would die. However, Satan told Eve she would not die if she ate from the tree but would be like God, knowing good and evil. In other words, instead of knowing the difference between good and evil which was established by God, she would know what was good and what was evil, in effect making herself her own god. Eve then ate from the tree and gave some of the fruit to her husband, and he also ate it.

God had established a boundary that divided good and evil. By eating the forbidden fruit, Adam and Eve encroached upon that boundary. One might liken God's boundary to a shopping aisle with Adam and Eve walking along the aisle choosing from either side. Because of the seemingly pleasantness of many sinful desires, they would have chosen much from the side of the boundary containing evil while declaring that it was good. They had fallen into Satan's trap without hope of escape. Unfortunately, this is the situation which many in this fallen world now find themselves. Because of the disobedience of Adam and Eve, God forbade them from eating from the tree of life and living forever. He banished them from the Garden of Eden and the perfect life they had known. Sin and death had entered the world.

Much is happening in our world today. The surrealistic times in which we are living have awakened an interest in God's word. Events occurring over several years have led to the reality we now face. However, the speed in which the final act has been played out in regard to our governmental system is frightening. America has fallen away from God, and America will pay the price. We know in our hearts the ways in which we have failed our Creator as a nation.

What can we expect now that we have turned from Him? Considering world events, I believe our only hope as a nation is a great revival that results in a return to God. The following passage of Scripture was written in regard to the Jewish people, but applies to today's Christians as well, for all believers are children of Abraham. "If my people, who are called by my name, will humble themselves and pray and seek my face and turn from their wicked ways, then will I hear from heaven and will forgive their sin and will heal their land." (2 Chronicles 7:14 NIV).

There are those who believe the world has become so filled with evil that we are nearing the end times. Only God knows when that will occur. Whether biblical scholar or layman, the Bible contains information that can seem overwhelming in regard to this subject. I will turn to the Bible for words of wisdom when considering the end of time: "Oh, the depth of the riches of the wisdom and knowledge of God! How unsearchable his judgements, and his paths beyond tracing out! Who has known the mind of the Lord? Or who has been his counselor?" (Romans 11:33-34 NIV).

In regard to the signs of the end of the ages, Jesus said, "No one knows about that day or hour, not even the angels in heaven nor the Son, but only the Father." (Matthew 24:36 NIV). While Jesus is God, there were self-imposed limitations in regard to His divine nature which had belonged to Him as the eternal Son. Thus, the human part of Jesus had no knowledge as to when these events would occur. However, even if He had known, Jesus probably would not have revealed the time because He wants us to remain watchful and focused on doing His work instead of giving over to idleness.

After His resurrection and victory over death, Jesus regained the entirety of His divine nature. In regard to current times, it might be years before the end time events start to occur so that more of humanity will have the opportunity to be drawn to God. On the other hand, it is possible the Rapture could occur before the things I am now writing can go through the various processes that are necessary for publication.

The terms and events associated with the end times are the Rapture, during which the dead bodies of all believers who had died over the generations will be resurrected and united with their spirits and souls which have been residing in Heaven. It will not matter about the decay of the bodies, for God will bring this about in a supernatural way. Then, all living believers will also be taken alive by Jesus to Heaven. This will include all infants and any child who has not reached the age of accountability. The Rapture will be that rising of the curtain for The Judgment Seat of God. This will be in regard to all who have accepted Christ, and will have nothing whatsoever to do with any losing their salvation. Salvation is a given, and can never be taken from one who has received God's grace.

The Judgement Seat of God will be conducted by Jesus, and awards will be given in accordance with each believer's service to God. Some will receive much, and some will receive little. Some will be asked why they did not do more, or why they were completely inactive in regard to their services to Him. During this occurrence, the believer will have the opportunity to communicate with Jesus on an individual basis. Our deepest yearnings to be close, to feel the love from, and worship the One who made us will be fulfilled.

The Rapture of believers brings in the seven-year Tribulation period on Earth for the multitudes that were left behind because of their refusal to repent. During this seven-year period, there will be much deceit and suffering upon the Earth, the likes of which have never before been experienced. During this terrible time, those who repent and turn to God will receive His forgiveness. However, many will continue on the path to destruction, choosing to follow the god of the world instead of the God of the universe.

The seven-year Tribulation will end because of the Second Coming of Jesus. All believers residing in Heaven, including those who experienced the Rapture, will accompany Christ to Earth. This is where they will now reside forever, because Earth, not Heaven, will be all believers' final home.

During the Second Coming, the devil will be bound by a great chain and thrown into the abyss for a thousand years. During this period of time, Jesus will rule on Earth with perfect justice and righteousness. After the thousand years have passed, the devil will be released for a short period of time. Even after the perfect rule of Jesus, the devil will entice some to attack

Israel. God will then destroy those attacking Israel with fire from the sky. And finally, The Great White Throne Judgment will occur. This is when Satan will meet his doom and be thrown into the lake of burning sulfur. All those who refused Jesus will receive the Judgment of eternal hell and separation from God. All evil will then have been eliminated, and the supremacy of God will prevail. There is a lot to digest in regard to the end times. These subjects should not be avoided when studying God's word. One thing is for certain, the born-again believers have every reason to rejoice and nothing to fear.

CHAPTER 13

"God formed man from the dust of the ground and breathed into his nostrils the breath of life, and the man became a living being." (Genesis 2:7 NIV). We are made in God's image and likeness. The wonderous reality of His presence would be more than sufficient, but there will be much more. God made us unique and we will remain so. We will be the same, but we will also be different, for we will be made perfect in His presence. He has been with us and will be with us forever. "Before I formed you in the womb, I knew you. Before you were born, I set you apart." (Jeremiah 1:5 NIV). Before conception and throughout our physical lives He is with us. God the Son suffered on the cross for the sins of humanity so there would be opportunity for life eternal. All that is required is the acceptance of the free gift God has offered all people, salvation from the penalty of sin through accepting Jesus as Lord and believing God raised him from death.

All people have one of two choices to make. Either God or Satan. What else is there? Certainly not self, for what can self hope to do when conscious thought ceases and the body decays? We do not have the power within us for anything more than that. Nor is there a magical man in the moon that will swoop down to the Earth whenever a person dies and carry that person to some magical everlasting paradise. We are either children of God or children of Satan. There is nothing else.

For those who have not yet accepted Christ and wish to do so, I will return to words I've previously written for they are words that warrant repetition. I am speaking of Paul's formula for receiving God's grace. "If you confess with your mouth Jesus is Lord, and believe in your heart that God raised Him from the dead, you will be saved. For it is with your heart that you believe and are justified, and it is with your mouth that you confess and are saved." (Romans 10:9-10 NIV).

What are the words one must use to benefit from this formula? It matters not, as long as you are sincere and the words are spoken from the heart. In your own words confess that you are a sinner, and ask for God's forgiveness. His forgiveness you will receive. It is the forgiveness of unconditional love. If you do this, your adventure with God will begin. It will never end.

God bless,

Burl L. Shepard

www.ingramcontent.com/pod-product-compliance
Lightning Source LLC
Chambersburg PA
CBHW031256120626
46545CB00007B/2842